FALL RISK

By the same author

Time Like Stone (UKZN Press, 2000)

Feet of the Sky (Brevitas Press, 2003)

Full Circle (Dye Hard Press, 2007)

Blind Voices: A Collection of Radio Plays (Botsotso, 2007)

Separating the Seas (UKZN Press, 2007)

Anatomy (Caversham Press, 2008)

Tilling the Hard Soil: Poetry and Prose by South African Writers Living with Disabilities (editor, UKZN Press, 2010)

Light and After (Deep South, 2010)

Left Over (Dye Hard Press, 2013)

A Book of Rooms (Deep South, 2014)

The Swimming Lesson and Other Stories (UKZN Press, 2017)

All and Everything (uHlanga, 2019)

The Mountain Behind the House (Dryad Press, 2020)

Notes from the Body: Health, Illness, Trauma (editor, w/ Duncan Brown and Nkosinathi Sithole, UKZN Press, 2023)

He Said // She Said (Dye Hard Press, 2024)

POEMS BY

Kobus Moolman

UHLANGA

2024

Fall Risk

© Kobus Moolman, 2024, all rights reserved

First published in Durban, South Africa by uHlanga in 2024

UHLANGAPRESS.CO.ZA

This edition is distributed outside of Southern Africa by the African Books Collective

AFRICANBOOKSCOLLECTIVE.COM

ISBN: 978-1-0370-0784-2

Edited by Nick Mulgrew
Cover illustration by Katherine Glenday
Cover design and typesetting by Nick Mulgrew
Proofread by Karina Szczurek

The body text of this book is set in Garamond Premier Pro
The cover and inside pages use Faust & Mephisto Regular and Italic

For Julia

with love

Soli Deo Gloria

POEMS

9

INDEX OF FIRST LINES

58

ACKNOWLEDGEMENTS

61

May I write words more naked than flesh,

stronger than bone, more resilient than sinew,

sensitive than nerve.

– SAPPHO

The body is twisted.

The body is tangled.

The body dissolves.

Always only the sky

and old stones left behind,

and the wind from a long way before.

☥

There are no islands in the sky.
There are no handles.
There are no dates in the sky.

Time is always everywhere
far behind everything else in the sky.

The moon and the sun switch on
at the same time in the sky.

The air is automatic.
The air is spontaneous.
The air is everywhere
the same size in the sky.

In the sky, the sky is anonymous.
In the sky, there is no sky.

The wind is drying out the sky,

    drying out the tears of the trees,

    the sweat of the mountains.

The wind is drying out the sodden

    trombone of the ocean,

    the thin serviette of the light.

The wind is drying out the darkness,

    drying out the smoke

    from the hundred fires lit

    to show God the way home.

Unable to think out loud, the man simply wrote
one word down after another, over and over
and again, so that from a distance the hills
merged, the bushes and the trees were
co-extensive, and the sound of rock
rusting was indistinguishable
from the sound of blood
beating against his
metallic skin.

†

Grab onto your hands.

Hold onto your hands.

Pull yourself up by your hands.

See your hands pulling.

See your hands holding

onto your hands.

See your hands grabbing

hold of your hands.

See your hands pulling you up

out of your old hands.

The strength of the sky
is failing. Its arms
so thin now, almost see-through.

The sky can no longer
hold its arms above its head.

It barely can discern
from which direction the future comes,
front or behind, east or west.

The sky is stalled
on the steep edge of destiny,
tilting away from the trees.

Away from the hope of the trees.

⚜

A sky   an eye.
  in the shape of

A mountain   a rope.
  in the shape of

A man   a hole.
  in the shape of

A woman   a fish.
  in the shape of

A floor   a pond.
  in the shape of

A bed   a ladder.
  in the shape of

The old writer likes to wear old clothes.

The old writer wears the same old clothes

all the time. The same broken old tracksuit top

night and day. Same old rag on his head.

Same and only pair of old boots.

Old black boots, all he ever has worn.

☦

Every day he feels himself to be a different man from the one he was the day before.

Just yesterday, the last day of the old year, he went to the bathroom in the seaside hotel where he and his wife were having lunch. He had already had three glasses of sweet white wine. And he looked at himself in the bright bathroom mirror that ran the length of the one wall. And he thought himself old and fat and ugly.

This morning he stumbled past the reflection of himself in the window of the small butchery. And he saw that he was indeed not the same man as yesterday. He was not younger or thinner of course. But there was definitely something different. Was it the flies crawling across his lips and across his shaved head? The crows croaking inside his mouth?

And now? Here? At this moment?

Now he looks down at his stiff and creaking hands. And he does not recognise them. They look like a rusted farm implement tossed into the veld behind a shed.

A strange implement for separating skin from flesh.

He does not know what to do
with himself. He is at a loss
to know which direction to go:
backwards, or backwards, or down.
He is sinking even when he is
standing still. His legs give in
even when he is lying down.
Lying to himself is the only option.
He is fine. Everything will be fine.
Just trust. God has a plan. Especially
for his body that keeps dropping
day by day its broken bits. He cannot
even write about it anymore, the slow
process of losing, losing, losing,
over and again, who he is.

In 1912 Egon Schiele was locked
up for twenty-four days in the
prison in the Austrian village
of Neulengbach (twenty miles
from Vienna) on charges of
immorality and seduction.

The painter wrote in his
prison diary: "Why? Why?
Why? I don't know."

And also: "How long
is it now that I have smelled
no cradling white winds
over swaying greenery?"

☥

On a worn-out sofa on the stoep of an old farmhouse
the man's black notebook pants and flaps
like a fish on dry land.

The man stares through the stiff plastic curtains
at the gum trees and the yellow hillside.

The clouds have been coming and going
all morning along the same narrow track of sky.

The man licks longing off the tips of his sour fingers.

The wind so very easily could be mistaken for a round sea.

But there is no wetness in the man's diet now,

nor is there forgetfulness. Here where who he is
there is barely even habit.

†

Does a heart beat still
here inside? the man asked,
as he banged the old wooden box,
the box that his grandfather stored
his old tools in, tools to repair
his heavy old black boots. And if,
if there is a heart here, he continued,
as he counted the loud feet
of the pedestrians, and counted
the loud feet of the old oak tree,
as he banged the old wooden box
of his ribcage, then can I, can I
can I still trust my blood,
can I still trust my old hands
to keep the lid tightly shut?

He picked every day
at the dry skin
in the palm of his hand
and the dry skin in-between
his cracked toes.

He pulled off long
strips of skin.

And he ate them:

like a magician
performing a vanishing act
in painstaking stages.

⚰

The earth is flat
without you,
the man read
to the woman.

The earth does not roll
through airless space
like a beach ball.

It slides slowly instead,
scraping its red arse
across the infinite
stony shore.

☦

Skin is a machine
for feeling things

the way needles do.

    Skin does not
    make a sound

    even turned inside out.

Skin is so tired
its glue comes undone

in the bath.

    Skin has to be
    carried everywhere

    it wants to go.

⚓

And so and so and because there was nowhere for him to put his legs his legs with his book open upon them he had to unclip them from the wall there where they were hooked zipper and rope and he had to fold them once twice this way then that left flap over right like a paper crane like a paper star a woman with all her thirst wrapped up and wet inside her plastic heart and he had to tie them up with the velcro strap this way then that and now his book had nowhere to put its arms and its old shoulder and there was nowhere for his eyes to go and he just had to hang there in the air like that like that like an old slow noose.

※

Day and night, night after night,
deep in his prayer, he deliberated whether
it was possible to draw the dark without ever looking at it.

He had his head in his hands.
His hands covered his eyes.
His breath caught on words that tasted like ash.

Day and night, night after night,
he dragged his slow feet across
the frozen lake of memory. It was dark always

beneath that bright film of appearances;
a darkness he trusted, the way a child
trusts his mother to recognise him in the rush after the bell.

Day and night, oh! night after night,
after so many mistakes, so many times around
and around the same stale track, he had begun to wonder

whether it ever would be possible to look –
only look – into the inside of that darkness,
without being turned into it.

☥

Now it is night again
and the stale static of insects and stars.

In the front yard the old oak tree
cradles its tired silence,

while birds in the ceiling
scratch through feathers and shit
to find their small sleep.

It is past the point where anything
will ever be able to go back
to what it was before.

We are walking
and we are crawling and falling,

all with our eyes sewn shut.

Unstitch me! Now,
here. Unpick me, quick!

The room shrinks into stillness.

The light of my bed-side lamp
stains the walls yellow.

There is a night just beyond the window
that these floral curtains keep out.

I am tired. My face is hot.
I have eaten too much sugar.

Drunk more coffee than I ought.

I am tired. And my face
is hot. And that rat is back in my side.

The night is just beyond the window.
And in the streets shadows crawl.

The room keeps coming up to me from below.

I am sitting upright in bed.

There is a rusted dog-chain
running from me to the edge of the stillness.

The light on the carpet is transparent.

I can see through it into the cold.

I am still tired. My face
is still hot. The rat is back:

the rat in my bladder and in my kidneys.

☨

The wind is a squeaking gate
that opens and shuts the tired eyes of the trees.

I watch the sky lower itself
like an old-fashioned lover onto the horizon.

A loud engine draws up alongside
the light dimming on the grass.

The engine runs on the same fuel
that jerks my legs and flickers across the page.

I cling onto the old fence that surrounds the light.
The trees and I breathe the same air as the stones.

⚘

Keep the sun on my bare head.
Keep the sun on my bare back
and on my chest and on my face.

Keep the shining sky always
in front of my eyes.

Keep the stony ground permanently
beneath my black boots.

The wind sits in-between the pages of this book
and the branches of the thin acacia trees,
covered with small yellow blossoms.

I seek no shade, no shelter
from these mountains and this sun.

I want to be stripped and dried out.
I want to be bleached as a bone.

I want to evaporate.

A woman stopped me this morning
as I was coming out of the doctor's surgery.
I had just received the news.
The woman said she had a pile
of poetry books for me in her car.
She'd been driving around for days
and days hoping to bump into me
somewhere in our small village.
I had just received the news
and so I wasn't feeling very talkative.
She dumped the box of books at my feet
and took off. Just like that.
Pictures of the Gone World,
The Death Notebooks.
Billy's Rain, by Hugo Williams,
about a woman's love affair with
a married man that goes sour.
But how did all these books know
where to find me, I wondered?
How did they know who I was?
At the bottom of the box there was even
a copy of one of my own books.
Leftover, I think it was.

Across the silent bay
the lights of the steelworks steam
as dawn ignites the kindling in the sky.

I have been stuck here all night
in this striped hotel chair, strung between
delirium and the glass boat of hope.

The sea is a lonely effort.

Like a waterfall it sits night and day
in the same old seat of stillness.

My pockets are weighted
down with tiredness. Salt
fills my pores.

Cold waves break over the sky.

A chair scrapes somewhere
in another room over and
again across a tiled floor.
I am on my back and
I am on my front.
There are whisperings too.
It is perhaps daylight already.
She has her hands splayed
like wild grass. But wildness
does not flourish anymore
where my hands touch.
Then the chair again. Then
the impact of crockery.
Then water that could be
heavy and dark. Or light. Inside
and out at the same time.

☦

"I spent a night with my beloved,"
Anaïs Nin writes in her diary.
But what does that short sentence mean?
Those seven words.
Seven is a sacred number.
It is supposed to be the number of God.
God finished his labours on the sixth day
and he rested on the seventh.

So what I want to know is
was the night that Anaïs Nin spent with her beloved
the night of the sixth or the seventh?

What I want to know is
was God alone when he rested?

☦

I burn easily, the man said.
Even in a flood.

It's always the eyes that go first.
Then the hair on the back of your neck.
And finally your skin that just can't stop.

And before you know it,
you're kneeling beside a dirty hotel bed,
and clamped around your head
a pair of arsonist's legs.

And everything, absolutely every
single thing underneath and behind and above and inside
and pressed right up against you

has melted

like hot glass.

Some mornings

I sit outside under the sun,

where the shadows dare not go,

when suddenly

for no reason whatsoever,

I am too afraid

to bend down

and lick up

even a single drop of my spit

from the stony ground.

☦

There are other voices inside my head now
and the sound of water rushing to get somewhere.

I can smell the colour red.
Words come out my mouth all sounding the same.

I do not know how to stop my fingers
repeating the same letters of the alphabet.

My hands do not know how to hold onto
anything anymore. Everything falls straight through.

I can feel everything inside of me
tilting over. It is happening now.

Now the sky is beneath my feet.
Now I look up toward the dark earth.

Along the dirt track behind the old stone church,
between the cypress trees and the overgrown graveyard,
where headstones kneel amongst broken bottles and shit,
a red wound runs.

The wound is as long
as the steeple sticking into the side of the sky.

It is a wound that will not close,
no matter the cure: sea water or spit, animal fat
or repentance.

It is a wound that keeps breaking open,
sliding the slippery insides of heaven out

for all of eternity.

☦

I cannot sit still
when I see the moon
sliding slowly through the clouds.

I want to throw something
at the black sky.
I want to drive out far
on a dirt road into the hills,
then turn around
and hurl myself at the moon.

I am all sick all over
of its perpetual beauty, its
remoteness on the hill.

I want flesh. I want skin.

I want something on my tongue
I can bite.

I am an animal
made of hands
and mouth.

I pant all over.

I am sticky
and I stink
of stickiness.

I lick everything.

Even the light
tastes of wet
and hungry.

Muddy lumps of organs.
Black dried blood. With flies.

The thick neck of an hyena tugs at old sinew.

And I wonder
whose stretched-white self-importance is this?

Whose belt? Whose rope?

Whose elastic to hold together
all of their hope?

The wind again is turning
all of the trees inside out.

Same wind that is slamming
every door shut behind me.

I no longer can use my arms
to walk or even roll.

And it is the same underbelly
of the sky as before and still.

Drilling down now
the only direction to go.

⚘

I am without a home.

> I have neither floor
> nor roof. Only fearful,
> lopsided letters like these
> to keep out the wind.

Only a dark rain.

> I have no straight line
> to close my eyes either. Only
> my mouth is my end.
> Only dark rain beneath

these strange low trees.

I am sitting all day
and I am sitting all night
on my hospital bed. I am not sick.
I am simply watching

and my mortality watches me
back. A small insect in a specimen
bottle. I am watching and waiting.
My waiting is a small key.

A small key that cannot see
where to fit into. I am sitting
and waiting for my mortality
to see where to take me.

All day and all night
I am sitting on my high bed.
Watching and waiting.
Impatient as an operating table.

There are holes in my feet
where the rain comes in.

And when I bend down to take off my legs
only the pattern of my socks remains.

There is a gap between the wind and the rain
in the shape of the cold.

And when I push up my arms
into the bottom of the ocean

only old sand is there.

⁂

I am made no longer
of the light made
in birds' beaks
or in bright leaves.

I am made now,
I see it, of the light made
in red stones, in silence
and in bright blades.

I am made no longer
to burn in the darkness
like a word. I am made now
of the darkness, and I burn

like a word.

That is not an owl
that calls there now.
That is the sound of a door
without an other side.

Those are not dogs howling.
Those are the hooves
of angels trampling
a dirt road into the night.

Even the tall windows
in the nave of the dark
know the hand-sign
for insubstantiality.

Even the lopsided trees
on the hillside
lean their thin rattles
away from the end.

And the final story is about
the man who could neither bend his back
nor turn his neck.

The man who could not stop leaking
cerebrospinal fluid from every orifice of his body.

The man who could not take a step
without wading through the thick sticky
liquid his body could neither keep in
nor stop producing.

The man at last whose only movements left
were those of his wide-open eyes

and his cracked tongue.

༊

Bare water.

Water without

exterior

except sound.

Bare water.

Water without

feeling

except doubt.

※

Index of first lines

The body is twisted ...	9
There are no islands ...	10
The wind is drying out ...	11
Unable to think out loud ...	12
Grab onto your hands ...	13
The strength of the sky ...	14

†

A sky in the shape of an eye ...	17
The old writer likes to wear ...	18
Every day he feels himself ...	19
He does not know what to do ...	20
In 1912 Egon Schiele ...	21
On a worn-out sofa ...	22
Does a heart beat still ...	23
He picked every day ...	24
The earth is flat ...	25
Skin is a machine ...	26
And so and so because ...	27
Day and night, night after night ...	28
Now it is night again ...	29
The room shrinks into stillness ...	30
The wind is a squeaking gate ...	32
Keep the sun on my bare head ...	33

†

A woman stopped me this morning ...	35
Across the silent bay ...	36
A chair scrapes somewhere ...	37
"I spent a night with my beloved," ...	38
I burn easily, the man said ...	39
Some mornings ...	40
There are other voices inside ...	41
Along the dirt track ...	42
I cannot sit still ...	43
I am an animal ...	44
Muddy lumps of organs ...	45
The wind again is turning ...	46
I am without a home ...	47
I am sitting all day ...	48
There are holes in my feet ...	49
I am made no longer ...	50

※

That is not an owl ...	53
And the final story ...	54
Bare water ...	55

※

Acknowledgements

Previous versions of these poems have been published in the *English Academy Review*, *New Contrast*, *New Coin*, *Stanzas* and *Five Points*.

Thanks to Robert Berold for his comments on early versions of the poems.

Thanks to Katherine Glenday for her beautiful cover art.

This book is dedicated to all the medical practitioners and nursing staff who have tended this mortal body throughout my life.

With my deepest respect and gratitude to Nick Mulgrew.

POETRY FOR THE PEOPLE

— RECENT RELEASES —

Dayspring: A Memoir by C. J. Driver, edited by J. M. Coetzee

The Book of Unrest by Nick Mulgrew

A Short Treatise on Mortality by Douglas Reid Skinner

Peach Country by Nondwe Mpuma
SHORTLISTED FOR THE 2023 NIHSS AWARD FOR BEST POETRY

Unam Wena ngu Mthunzikazi A. Mbungwana

Jesus Thesis and Other Critical Fabulations by Kopano Maroga
SHORTLISTED FOR THE 2022 NIHSS AWARD FOR BEST POETRY

— RECENTLY-AWARD-WINNING TITLES —

Ilifa ngu Athambile Masola
WINNER OF THE 2022 NIHSS AWARD FOR BEST POETRY

An Illuminated Darkness by Jacques Coetzee
WINNER OF THE 2022 INGRID JONKER PRIZE
WINNER OF THE 2022 OLIVE SCHREINER PRIZE

All the Places by Musawenkosi Khanyile
WINNER OF THE 2021 NIHSS AWARD FOR BEST POETRY
WINNER OF THE 2020 SOUTH AFRICAN LITERARY AWARD FOR POETRY

Everything is a Deathly Flower by Maneo Mohale
WINNER OF THE 2020 GLENNA LUSCHEI PRIZE FOR AFRICAN POETRY

Zikr by Saaleha Idrees Bamjee
WINNER OF THE 2020 INGRID JONKER PRIZE

AVAILABLE FROM GOOD BOOKSTORES IN SOUTHERN AFRICA
& FROM THE AFRICAN BOOKS COLLECTIVE ELSEWHERE

UHLANGAPRESS.CO.ZA

www.ingramcontent.com/pod-product-compliance
Lightning Source LLC
Chambersburg PA
CBHW071013160426
43193CB00012B/2033